BIG LITTLE TALKS

TALKS

A SEX-POSITIVE APPROACH FOR PARENTING

MICHAEL GENE

EDITED BY
LAURA ELIZABETH

THIRD EDITION

ISBN
979-8-9879431-2-0
979-8-9879431-3-7 (ebook)
979-8-9879431-4-4 (audiobook)

To my lovely daughter

Put a little light on the subject

CONTENTS

FORWARD

Talking with your kids about sex can promote enjoyable, healthy, and happy experiences in their future and safeguard them from doing something they'll regret. No one has more influence on kids' decision-making than parents, and when you provide them with accurate information, you empower your kids to navigate the complex choices involved in becoming sexually active.

Many young people engage in sexual behavior prematurely before their brains have fully developed and they understand the risks. This can lead to painful and emotionally damaging situations. Teaching our kids a clear understanding of consent and how to approach sexuality in a healthy way, before they begin having sexual experiences, may help them avoid going through that.

When your children are as young as preschool age, you can begin by naming body parts accurately and teaching them about personal boundaries and privacy. As your kids grow older, you can have more detailed conversations about relationships, responsibilities, resisting sexual pressure, and enjoying sex safely.

This book is meant to provide inspiration to help you

get this important conversation started with your own kids. Talking about sex is best done over time with lots of little talks as opposed to one big talk. Let's teach our kids sensible information they can use to stay healthy and to find enjoyment in all aspects of their lives, including sexuality.

SCRIPTS TO GET TALKS STARTED

WHERE DO BABIES COME FROM?

Little puppies are so adorable, right? You probably know that the **female*** dog has the puppies, but did you ever wonder how the puppies got inside of her? The way that happens is a **male** dog will get really close to the female dog and they will physically join their bodies together. The male dog will put a part of his body, which sticks out from it, into the part of the female dog, which is like a tube that goes into her. This physical act of joining their bodies together is called having **sex** and the female dog can get **pregnant** with puppies from doing this. The word sex can also be used when you want to know the **gender** of someone, like when you ask whether a person is a boy or a girl.

People, just like dogs and other animals, are also capable of reproducing themselves by having sex, getting pregnant, and making babies. This is how babies are born. If you have any questions about any of this and I don't know the answer, let's try to find it out together.

*Bolded words appear in the Words section starting on pg. 33

OUR AMAZING BODIES

So now that we have an idea of what sex is and know that animals, including people, have it, let's talk more about our bodies. People have special parts of their bodies that they use for sex. These parts are called **genitals**. It is very rare, but sometimes humans are born with genitals that are not completely male or female, and this is called **intersex**. However, most often baby boys are born with male genitals and baby girls with female genitals. The genitals consist of both external and internal parts and are the human **reproductive organs**. A girl's external genitals are made up of the **vulva**, which includes the two sets of **labia** that open to the **vagina** and **clitoris**. A boy's external genitals are made up of a **penis** and the **testicles**. The genitals are the parts of the human body that are joined together when humans have sex for reproduction.

Even though babies are born with reproductive organs and genitals, they are unable to have sex and reproduce yet. Their bodies have to mature and go through important changes later in life as they grow into an adult. You may be curious about your body and others' bodies and this is very normal. It is common for kids younger than age seven to explore by "**playing doctor**." Experts usually agree that playing like this can be an innocent way to learn about our bodies as long as: everyone is close in age, wants to play, and is motivated by curiosity only and no one gets hurt, touched in a way they do not want, or inserts anything into a body opening. This can be an opportunity to learn about **personal privacy** and **respecting others**.

It is never okay for someone to touch you in a way that you do not want to be touched or to make you do something you do not want to do. Nor is it okay for you to touch someone in a way that they do not want to be touched or to make someone do something that they do not want to do. Also, know that adults should never touch a young person in a sexual way or even talk about doing that. It is very wrong and illegal if they do. If an adult acts like this, it is not the fault of the child and it needs to be reported to a parent or another trusted adult. It may be difficult to talk about a situation like that, but it must not be kept a secret and has to stop immediately.

It is very important that you understand that your body is yours alone and no one can decide what you do with it except you. This is called **body sovereignty** and that means you have complete control over it.

OUR GROWING BODIES

Young bodies need to mature and go through changes before they are able to have sex and reproduce. When your body is going through these changes, it is referred to as **puberty**. You may notice that your friends' bodies are changing, too, and maybe at a different time and in different ways than yours is. This is completely normal. Puberty begins at different times for everyone, but girls usually experience puberty between ages 8 and 13, ending by the time they turn 15, and boys typically experience it between ages 10 and 14, ending by the time they turn 16. Some of the first noticeable physical changes girls experience is that their **breasts** will begin to grow, and they will start to develop **pubic hair**. Hair will also grow in their armpits and may get thicker and darker in other places on the body. Girls will also begin to have a **period** and have **vaginal discharge** and **vaginal lubrication**. Some of the first noticeable physical changes in boys going through puberty is that their testicles will get bigger and they will start to develop pubic hair, as well as armpit and facial hair. Their voice may crack sometimes as it starts to change and get deeper. They will also begin to have more frequent **erections**.

Both boys and girls may **masturbate** before puberty begins and may continue doing so after it has. This activity is always to be done in private. The pleasure they feel from touching their own genitals during masturbation may cause them to have an **orgasm**. Both boys and girls may also experience **wet dreams**.

It is also common for some boys and girls to develop **acne** on their skin due to the release of **hormones** during puberty. The hormones that the brain releases send signals to your body to make the physical changes you see on the outside. They also affect the internal emotions you feel. You may start to have new, exciting, and sometimes confusing emotions. You may develop a **crush** on someone and **desire** to spend time with that person. Sometime later in puberty, you may become curious about **romantic** and **sexual relationships** for the first time.

The period of going through the physical and emotional changes of transitioning out of childhood into adulthood is your **adolescence**. All of this change is about getting the body ready for reproduction and starting to become an adult.

> "... give sex itself the breathing room to become a mundane, safe, everyday topic as normal as homework or soccer practice or weather."
>
> — Bonnie J. Rough
>
> *Beyond Birds and Bees,* 2018

WHAT IS SEX?

Many parents find it difficult to talk with their kids about sex, but talking helps better prepare you for **sexual activity** when you are ready to experience it. It is much better to learn from your parents than from your friends, television shows, or the Internet. We can talk openly and discuss any questions you may have so you are well educated and able to make good decisions for yourself. After you have gone through all of the emotional and physical changes of puberty and become an adult, sexual activity is something very exciting and wonderful to look forward to. It is a completely natural part of the human experience and can be one of the most important aspects of your life physically and emotionally. However, there is a lot to learn in order to be safe and healthy with sexual activity, and this is why it is best to wait until you are an adult. Before a person has sex, she or he is considered a **virgin**. Before becoming sexually active, you should know that all types of sexual activity have risks and need to be done responsibly. When people have sex for reproduction they will have **sexual intercourse**, which involves the penis going inside of the vagina. (Some people may need to go to a doctor for help getting pregnant or they may adopt a child instead.) Besides reproduction, people have sex for another reason, too, and that is for **pleasure**. Sex can feel really great. Sexual activity done for pleasure only can include **French kissing**, **oral sex**, **mutual masturbation** and **anal sex**. For sex to be a great experience, it is important that both sexual partners believe it is done at the right time and for the right reasons.

WHAT YOU SHOULD KNOW ABOUT SEX

Sex Is Private

All types of sexual activity are very private and need to be done in a safe and comfortable place. Even talking about sex is best kept private and respectful.

The Best Time For Sex

The best time for sex is when it is shared between two mature people that are in a respectful, trusting and loving relationship. This is what is referred to as **love making** and there is no better way to enjoy sex than like this.

Sex Needs To Be Agreed To

When you have become mature enough for sexual activity, the decision to begin having sex is yours alone and no one else can decide for you. It is a very personal decision and others have the same right to decide for themselves. No one should ever be forced or pressured into sex. Remember that "no" means "no" and only a very clear and coherent "yes" (from someone not under the influence of drugs and/or alcohol) can mean "yes." Also, keep in mind that a person always has the right to change "yes" to "no" at any time throughout a sexual encounter.

If someone is trying to get you to do something that you do not want to do, it is important to skillfully protect yourself. Learn to use **refusal skills** such as explaining why you want them to stop, using body language like putting a hand up, suggesting doing something else instead, or taking action like getting up and leaving. You need to get to a safe environment immediately if someone isn't taking "no" for an answer.

On the other hand, if you are trying to get someone to

do something they do not want to do, you need to stop immediately. When you force or coerce someone into sex, you are committing a crime and can find yourself in very real trouble. It will end up hurting you as well and fill you with painful guilt and shame. It also puts your chances of enjoying future sexual experiences at risk. Instead of making someone do something they do not want to do, go be alone and masturbate. Sex with another person will only be truly enjoyable and positive if you both agree to it.

Sex Is A Serious Activity

Having sex is a serious activity and it is important to understand the potential consequences before deciding to become sexually active. There are real risks to having sex. It is possible to catch a **sexually transmitted disease** when having sex, even ones that may eventually kill you. The risk of **unplanned pregnancy** also comes with having sex. There are different types of **contraceptives** available to help prevent pregnancy. Wearing a **condom** may help prevent not only pregnancy but also disease, so it is very important to use one when having sex. However, the only 100% way to prevent these risks is not to have sex at all. When you choose not to have sex this is called **abstinence**.

Go At Your Own Pace

You may learn that some of your friends have had sex before you. Sometimes people feel **peer pressure** to do something because others are and you want to fit in and be accepted. But it is best to wait until you know you are completely ready and really want to. Everyone goes at their own pace, and it is okay to go at yours.

The First Time

It is normal to feel a little afraid of doing something for the first time and that includes having sex. During sexual intercourse you may experience some pain and/or it may feel good. Girls have a **hymen** that partially closes the opening of the vagina and the first time a penis or a finger goes inside, the hymen may stretch and cause some pain and bleeding. There may also be pain during sex if the vagina isn't wet enough with lubrication. Take your time and use **foreplay** before beginning to have sexual intercourse. This will build up the anticipation and enhance the experience. It is important for you and your partner to be relaxed and wait until you are completely ready. During sex be sure to communicate clearly about what feels good and what doesn't. If something hurts, then stop. Instead of having intercourse, one way to continue might be to use your hand to touch the genitals of your partner. Sex should ultimately feel good and be very comfortable.

The Right Partner Makes All the Difference

It is important to choose the right **sexual partner**. Take time to get to know that person really well and make sure you like doing other things with them like talking, going on walks, watching movies, attending concerts, sharing meals, holding hands, and hanging out with friends together. If you feel comfortable with them and never pressured to do something that you don't want, then that can be a very good sign. Look for someone interested in more than just sex. A loving, sexual relationship can be a wonderful part of a life that is filled with a variety of healthy activities, but sex alone isn't enough to make your life interesting and fulfilling.

Real Life Change

What other people tell you and what you see in movies, on television, and online about sex isn't always realistic. Being in a sexual relationship with someone will bring real changes to your lives. You will feel new emotions that can be very strong, and you may find it hard to focus on anything but your relationship. Learn to balance your life and take care of important responsibilities. Concentrate on being the best person you can be and it will be easier to establish a good relationship with someone else.

As wonderful as being in a relationship can be, there can also be situations that cause suffering. When a person has sex with someone other than the person they are in a relationship with, this is called **cheating**. It is very painful and disrespectful. Also, some relationships eventually end and this can be a difficult time for both of you. **Breaking up** with someone is serious and deserves more attention than just doing it over a text or telling a friend to convey the message. Be as respectful as possible to one another. Stay in touch with your own feelings, and be considerate to the feelings of others, too. Everyone can experience **heartbreak** at some point, but the pain you feel will be less and less as time goes on.

If someone has no interest in a relationship with you, you may experience a feeling of **rejection**. Their reasons could have nothing to do with you, but regardless you must respect their privacy. Overtime it will no longer seem like such a big deal. Stay positive and focus instead on going forward and meeting someone that shares mutual feelings with you.

Avoid Unhealthy Sexuality

Participating in "**hookup culture**" where people meet with someone for no other reason but **casual sex** is wise to avoid. This behavior puts you at risk emotionally and physically. Even without any expectations of starting a relationship, it can still be painful if the other person ghosts you and acts as if nothing ever happened. You can end up feeling empty, regretful, and depressed from being used or guilty because you used somebody else. This activity can increase the chances of contracting a sexually transmitted disease, unplanned pregnancy, and/or sexual assault, especially with alcohol and drugs being involved.

It is common for high school girls to be interested in relationships while high school boys are mostly interested in just sex. This could be part of a developmental stage and an example of girls maturing faster, but the sooner boys mature the better. The irony is that when they begin to focus less on their own sexual gratification and more on their partner's, the more enjoyment they end up having.

There are ways of being sexual even without physically being with someone else that are very unhealthy. **Pornography** is more easily accessible now more than at any other time in history, so no wonder it has become such an issue for so many of us. Looking at porn can become addictive, get in the way of achieving your goals, and be a real time suck. Instead of wasting valuable time on it, you could be practicing to become better at a sport, studying for an exam, helping a friend out, learning a musical instrument, reading, spending time developing a real-life relationship, or any number of other healthy activities. Sex shown in porn is done by actors and is often fantasized, so what you see is an unnatural interaction between people. Learning sex from porn can lead to high-risk sexual behavior and give you unrealistic ideas on how you are supposed to look, act, sound, and perform. One sex scene can be filmed over a long period of time and then edited down to make it look as though everything went perfectly. When you compare your sexual performance with what you see in porn, you may start to feel inadequate. Real-life encounters are much more complex and exciting than viewing others having sex on screen. Some times sex may end up being less than perfect, and that is okay. The important thing is the connection you share with the other person. Being sexy is an attitude, not a specific type of body size or shape. Often people in porn have had surgeries to alter their bodies. Also, the size of a penis can vary a lot. More important than size is how in-tune you are with your partner during sex and how you respond to what they want and like.

Perhaps the reason that hookup culture and watching porn are so prevalent today is due to a fear of and aversion to "catching feelings." While it may be easier to masturbate to porn and seem safer to avoid starting a relationship, no experience with porn or a casual hookup can ever match the pleasure and excitement you will feel from connecting emotionally and sexually with another human being in a genuine, consensual, and respectful way. Yes, there may be some pain from a relationship that fails to work out, but this is a part of the human experience that will help you grow and learn what you ultimately want in a partner. So take a chance: look someone in the eye and take the time to start a real-life relationship.

Sexting or posting sexual messages or **nude** photos can be damaging, painful, and embarrassing. Even those sent to someone you trust in private can be made public accidentally or intentionally. It is impossible to delete these things and the damage can be long-term. It is best to keep your posts and messages non-sexual. Also be aware that **cyber predators** may contact you online pretending to be someone else and using fake profile pictures. They may flatter you, tell you lies in order to gain your trust, talk about sex, want nude photos and/or ask to meet. Always be on your guard when online and never share personal information or agree to meet with someone.

Different Beliefs

People have many different beliefs about sex. Some believe you should wait to have sex until you are married. Some people decide not to have sex at all. Some people are **heterosexual** and prefer to be with the opposite gender. Some people are **homosexual** and have sex with the same gender, like a man with a man or a woman with a woman. It is important to know what is right for you and at the same time respect and be sensitive to the beliefs of others.

WRONG AND/OR HARMFUL SEX

Sexual Assault/Abuse – when someone does a sexual act against someone without the other person agreeing to it

Molestation – inappropriate touching, looking, pestering and/or harassing that is unwanted from someone

Rape – when someone forces someone without their consent and with or without violence to have sexual intercourse; can be done by a stranger or someone you know

Other types/situations:

> **Date Rape** – when a rape is done by someone the victim knows
>
> **Statutory Rape** – when an adult has sex with someone who is not old enough and under the legal age of consent
>
> **Date Rape Drugs** – drugs which can be given to you in a drink or food without your being aware of it; can cause you to be unable to say "no" to unwanted sex and not remember everything that happened

All types of rape, sexual assault, and molestation are illegal and have serious consequences. They should be reported to a trusted adult and the police immediately. These acts can happen at school, church, home, etc., and can be done by other kids or adults.

Accidental Pregnancy – when someone gets pregnant without planning or wanting to be; can cause a lot of difficulty for both people, such as having to make a tough decision like **abortion** or adoption. Condoms and other contraceptives are good at preventing pregnancy, but no contraceptive offers 100% protection

STD and **STI** – sexually transmitted disease and sexually transmitted infection; can cause pain, discomfort, embarrassment, illness, and death. Condoms are good at preventing most infections so use them every time

Infidelity (cheating) – when someone in a relationship has sex with someone other than their partner; this is an unfaithful action that can be very painful for your spouse or partner

Alcohol and Drugs – alcohol and drugs complicate sex; thinking can become clouded and make it difficult for you to make the right decision, resulting in risky, unsafe behavior and/or sexual assault. The effects may feel fun in the moment, but when they wear off you will have to face the reality of your actions or what has happened

SEX CAN BE WONDERFUL

Reproduction – sex can allow for new babies to be born!

Pleasure – sex can provide wonderful feelings both emotionally and physically

Bonding – when two mature people care for one another and want to feel closer, having healthy sexual relations can help them be more connected

Health benefits – healthy and safe sexual activities can benefit your immune system, provide stress relief, improve sleep, and boost health in other ways

Exercise – sexual activity takes energy and can be a way to get more exercise

Self Esteem Boost – being in a healthy, consensual and caring sexual relationship can help a person feel great about themselves

PRE-SEX CHECKLIST

1. You have gotten to know the other person really well and have met their family and/or friends

2. Neither of you is in another relationship

3. You will have the privacy you deserve in a place that is safe and comfortable

4. You have a plan in case an unintended pregnancy happens

5. You know that you can change your mind at any time and that there are other types of sexual contact that can still be satisfying and be safer than intercourse

6. You understand that this new activity may be very exciting, but you still need to focus on taking care of your other responsibilities

7. You and your partner are mature enough to responsibly honor the three must knows before having sex *(see next chapter)*

THREE MUST-KNOWS BEFORE HAVING SEX

1. Both you and your partner really want to have sex and there is no pressure to do it

2. Both you and your partner know how to protect against sexually transmitted diseases

3. Both you and your partner know how to protect against unwanted pregnancy

SECRET TO GREAT SEXUAL EXPERIENCES

Here is the secret to having great sexual experiences (boys, this is especially important for you): focus on making sure your partner enjoys it and seek ways to bring them pleasure. You will end up finding more pleasure for yourself! It is very important that your partner does the same. Sex should always be treated as a shared experience to be celebrated and never as a selfish act. Communicate openly with your partner during sex about what you like and don't like and listen to what her or his needs are.

Also, after sex, spend some time **cuddling** with your partner. This will give the **intimacy**, **attraction**, and **appreciation** you share with your partner a chance to grow and become stronger. Not only that, but this will increase the likelihood that you continue enjoying the experience with your partner and more often.

WORDS

Female – a living being that may give birth to babies, such as a woman

Male – a living being that may get a female pregnant, such as a man

Pregnant – when a living being has a baby growing inside of it

Reproduction – when a living being makes a baby of itself

Sex – a physical and emotional act that may involve feeling sexual pleasure

Gender – identifying as male or female or other

Genitals – a living being's sexual organs

Intersex – having characteristics that do not fit typical definitions for male or female bodies

Reproductive Organs – a living being's body parts related to sexual reproduction

Vulva – female external genitals; includes the opening to the vagina, the clitoris, the two sets of labia and the urethra

Labia – the inner and outer folds of skin of the vulva that protect the other external genitals

Vagina – a part of a female's genitals which is sensitive to sexual pleasure; the tube leading from the external genitals into the female body and what the penis enters during sexual intercourse; in natural childbirth, babies come out of the female here

Clitoris – a highly sensitive area of the genitals of a woman that can bring great sexual pleasure

Penis – a part of a male's genitals which is sensitive to sexual pleasure; it grows into an erection and enters the vagina of a woman during sexual intercourse

Testicles – areas of the male genitals where sperm is made

"Playing Doctor" – a phrase used to refer to children examining the genitals of each other out of curiosity; originates from children using the pretend roles of doctor and patient

Personal Privacy – the ability and right to keep something about yourself hidden from others

Respecting Others – treating and thinking about others with kindness

Body Sovereignty – you are the only one to have control over your own body

Puberty – the physical and emotional changes a young person goes through while transitioning from a child into an adult that may be capable of making babies

Breasts – the soft raised areas on a female's chest that include nipples, which are sensitive to sexual pleasure and can be used for a mother to feed her children breast milk

Pubic Hair – the hair that starts to grow around the genitals during puberty

Period – a normal, healthy event that occurs about once a month to adolescent girls and women who are not pregnant; the blood that would have been used to nourish a growing baby sheds out of the vagina for about a week, causing cramps and other physical and emotional discomfort

Vaginal Discharge – natural and normal fluid released from the vagina to keep it clean and help prevent infection

Vaginal Lubrication – the wetness inside of the vagina caused by sexual arousal and anticipation of sexual activity

Erection – a penis that has become larger and hard due to sexual arousal and anticipation of sexual activity

Masturbation – the act of a person giving themselves sexual pleasure by touching their own genitals, which is a natural way to explore and learn about your body; can be a safe and healthy way to release sexual urges

Orgasm – the extreme point of pleasure that comes during sexual activity

Wet Dreams – a dream about sex that is pleasurable and sometimes results in an orgasm

Hormones – chemicals released from your brain that cause changes to your body and feelings

Crush – a feeling of strong attraction to someone

Desire – a strong feeling that you really want something

Romantic – feeling love for someone and acting in a way to show it

Sexual Relationships – sharing sexual activity with someone

Adolescence – the time of transitioning from being a child and turning into an adult

Sexual Activity – acts that usually involve the genitals and feeling sexual pleasure

Virgin – typically refers to someone who has never had sexual intercourse; some may consider themselves no longer a virgin due to another sexual activity

Sexual Intercourse – a sexual act that involves penetration, especially the inserting of a penis inside a vagina; may be used for reproduction

Pleasure – a sensation and feeling that feels really good to you physically and emotionally

French Kissing – kissing which involves contact between tongues

Oral sex – when a person uses their mouth on the genitals of another person to give them sexual pleasure; carries the same risks of disease as sexual intercourse

Mutual masturbation – when people touch their own genitals or each other's for sexual pleasure; can be safer than other types of sexual activity when no bodily fluids are exchanged and can be a good alternative to sexual intercourse when someone is not ready for that

Anal Sex – a sexual act that generally involves a penis being inserted inside the anus

Refusal Skills – a set of skills designed to help children avoid participating in behaviors they are being pressured into

Sexually Transmitted Disease – an infection transmitted during sexual contact that can be caused by a virus, bacteria or parasite

Condom – something put over an erect penis during sex to help prevent pregnancy and disease

Abstinence – choosing not to do something, especially have sex

Peer Pressure – when you feel like you should do something because others are trying to get you to do it or because you feel you need to do it to fit in

Hymen – the thin layer of skin that partially covers the opening of the vagina

Foreplay – types of sexual activity that happen before sexual intercourse such as kissing and touching

Sexual Partner – the person you are sharing sexual activity with

Cheating – when someone you have an established sexual relationship with betrays you by having sex with someone else

Breaking Up – when people decide to put an end to

their relationship

Heartbreak – a painful feeling when a relationship you have been in or still want to be in is over

Rejection – a painful feeling when someone turns you down for a date or relationship

Hookup Culture – unhealthy behavior of meeting with others for casual sex only

Pornography – images and videos that include others doing sexual acts

Sexting – a text message that is about sex or includes sexual photos

Nude – when a body has no clothing

Cyber Predators – strangers that use the Internet to prey on kids in a sexual way

Heterosexual – preferring to have sexual relations with the opposite sex

Homosexual – preferring to have sexual relations with the same sex

Cuddling – holding someone close to show love and affection

Intimacy – being very close to someone physically and emotionally

Attraction – a strong feeling of being drawn to someone

Appreciation – being grateful for and enjoying the qualities of someone

Sexual Arousal – when a person feels ready for sexual activity

Erogenous zones – areas of your body that when touched cause sexual arousal

Ejaculation – when semen comes out of a penis during an orgasm

Sperm – the special type of cell carried in semen that causes pregnancy

Egg – the special cell in a woman that when a sperm enters it, the woman becomes pregnant

Consent – someone agreeing to do something, such as a sexual act

Boundary – your limit for what you are comfortable doing, which only you - and no one else - can decide to change

Sexual Health – a positive, safe and respectful approach to any kind of sexual act

Private Parts – areas of your body that a typical bathing suit covers up

Casual Sex – sexual activity without emotional intimacy between people who are not established partners; can also be referred to as "empty sex"

Promiscuous – having casual sexual relationships with many different people

Circumcision – a medical procedure sometimes done to baby boys to remove the foreskin of the penis

Abortion – a medical procedure to end a pregnancy; can be challenging to go through emotionally and/or physically

Contraceptive – a method used to avoid pregnancy

Hickey – a mark that looks sort of like a bruise caused by sucking on the skin

Sexual predator – a person that sexually assaults another

Sexual offender – a person who commits a crime involving sex

Lust – a very strong sexual desire

Libido – the sexual desire a person feels

Slang terms related to sex – disrespectful, impolite, and improper words that are best to avoid such as: male slut, slut, cunt, titties, pussy, dick, boning, boner, blow job, screwing, shagging, going down, getting laid, etc.

ACKNOWLEDGMENTS

Thank you to my family and friends that provided feedback and/or help while this book was being written.

ADDITIONAL RESOURCES

amaze.org

bonniejrough.com

getrealeducation.org

healthychildren.org

ncsby.org

peggyorenstein.com

sexedrescue.com

whysexed.org

learningcourage.org

Love...
rejoices with the truth... always
protects, trusts, hopes, and perseveres.

– 1 Corinthians 13